What Time Is It?

by Jeanette Mara
illustrated by Stacey Schuett

HARCOURT BRACE & COMPANY

Orlando Atlanta Austin Boston San Francisco Chicago Dallas New York
Toronto London

What time is it?
Time to eat, squirrel.

What time is it?
Time to eat, Baby.

What time is it?